INTERMEDIATE PIECES

FOR**CLASSICAL**GUITAR

20 Beautiful Classical Guitar Pieces to Build Your Repertoire

ROB**THORPE**

FUNDAMENTAL**CHANGES**

Intermediate Pieces for Classical Guitar

20 Beautiful Classical Guitar Pieces to Build Your Repertoire

Published by www.fundamental-changes.com

ISBN 978-1-78933-008-3

www.fundamental-changes.com

Twitter: **@guitar_joseph**

Over 10,000 fans on Facebook: **FundamentalChangesInGuitar**

Instagram: **FundamentalChanges**

For over 250 Free Guitar Lessons with Videos Check Out

www.fundamental-changes.com

Cover Image Copyright: ShutterStock Melis

Contents

Foreword

Welcome to the second of my two classical guitar books which aim to build your repertoire as a solo performer.

When people hear that you are a musician, they often say, "Well, play something then!" This book will prepare you to do just that. Continuing where book one left off, this volume will help you expand your classical guitar repertoire and further develop the essential skills of fingerpicking and chord playing.

The pieces here have been carefully selected to build on the foundations laid in book one (First Pieces for Classical Guitar). There is common ground between the two volumes, but the music presented here demands a slightly higher level of technical skill. There are faster passages to play, more challenging chord shapes to master, and some new techniques to learn.

Additionally, this book features longer pieces with more complex structures and frequent dynamic transitions to give light and shade. Some of the pieces also make use of altered tunings, which I will explain as we come to them.

Some of the music here is drawn from the canon of Classical era guitar music, such as by Carulli and Carcassi, as well as Romantic composers like Tárrega. You will also tackle a few pieces originally written for piano that have been arranged for guitar, and some original pieces I've written especially for this book. The latter were inspired by two different approaches to steel string guitar playing.

As you work through the book, break each piece down into sections and make sure you are comfortable with the technical challenges each section presents before you work on performing the piece as a whole. That said, this book has been created to encourage you to perform, and love the music you play. It's about performance, not just practice!

I hope you enjoy playing this music and find it rewarding to study.

Enjoy the journey!

Rob

Practice and Performance Tips

Throughout the book I will suggest picking and fingering patterns. Picking hand digits will be marked with the following letters: **P** = thumb; **I** = index; **M** = middle; **A** = ring. Fretting hand fingerings will be marked above the notation by the numbers 1-4, with 1 being the index finger and 4 being the pinkie.

Occasionally I will refer to playing in a particular *position* on the fretboard. The position number indicates where your index finger should rest on the fretboard. E.g. "Play this in fourth position" means your index finger will be placed across the 4th fret.

This book is intended to be a collection of performance pieces. Each piece has an accompanying explanation, but I don't set out to teach you how to play the piece in minute detail. I do, however, explain how to tackle the technical challenges each piece presents. If you need more input, I suggest working through this repertoire alongside a dedicated technique method, or with a local teacher.

In book one we discussed the use of *free stroke* and *rest stroke*. To recap, free stroke involves pulling the string out slightly as you pluck it. Rest stroke pushes the finger/thumb "through" the string, so that it ends up resting against the adjacent string. Some of the pieces in this book will especially benefit from the use of rest stroke. Rest stroke gives a more strident sound which helps to emphasis a melody. Free stroke should be used when several strings are to ring out together.

Tone and instrument choice

When it comes to producing the authentic tone of the classical guitar, there is no substitute for the nails of your picking hand to get the tone spot on. Unfortunately, having long nails doesn't lend itself to other types of guitar playing (mainly electric guitar) and filing them to get the best connection with the string becomes a regular chore. Alternatively, there are ranges of synthetic "fake" nails available instead, or you can use the flesh of your fingertips for a warmer, quieter tone.

Regarding your choice of instrument: any decent acoustic guitar will do, but a Spanish classical guitar will provide the most authentic sound. A steel strung acoustic will lend a more folky interpretation to the pieces. Personally, I enjoy the sound of classical fingerstyle applied to the electric guitar. Experimenting with chorus effects or very subtle amounts of overdrive can give an exciting new spin to pieces written more than a hundred years before the electric guitar was invented!

Above all, experiment, find your own sound and enjoy playing the pieces.

Get the Audio

The audio files for this book are available to download for *free* from **www.fundamental-changes.com** and the link is in the top right corner. Simply select this book title from the drop-down menu and follow the instructions to get the audio.

We recommend that you download the files directly to your computer, not to your tablet and extract them there before adding them to your media library. You can then put them on your tablet, iPod or burn them to CD. On the download page there is a help PDF and *we also provide technical support through the form on the download page.*

We spend a long time getting the audio just right and you will benefit greatly from listening to these examples as you work through the book. They're free, so what are you waiting for?!

Head over to **www.fundamental-changes.com** and grab the audio files now.

There are also over 200 free guitar lessons you can get your teeth into.

1. Minuet from Sonata No. 34 in D – Joseph Haydn
(arranged by Francisco Tárrega)

Franz Joseph Haydn (1732-1809) was an Austrian composer of prolific output. In addition to being important to the development of the symphony and string quartet forms, he composed fifty-one keyboard sonatas during his lifetime.

The piece presented here is an arrangement of the minuet movement from his thirty-fourth sonata. The minuet is a dance in 3/4 time. It differs from the waltz due to its characteristic pickup beat and the bouncy dotted quaver/semiquaver rhythm on each beat. Each beat in a bar has the same emphasis, as opposed to the strong second and third beats that define the waltz.

This particular arrangement is the first of several featured by respected composer and guitarist Francisco Tárrega. Rather than transcribing the whole piece, Tárrega opted to cut Haydn's minuet down to its two most memorable melodic phrases, which open the piece and then reappear towards the end of the original work.

This arrangement calls for Drop D tuning. This simply means retuning the low E string down a tone to D. The result is that we can keep the music in its original key, but enjoy a rich, resonant low root note, as heard in bars one and eight.

Use your second finger for the high D in bar one. The stretch with fingers three and fourth on beat 2 means the first finger is free to barre the 2nd fret for the A Major chord in the next bar.

Keep a moderate pressure as you slide your fourth finger from the 5th to 8th fret. The pressure should come from pulling your arm back from the elbow and maintaining a strong form in the fretting finger. The thumb shouldn't be squeezing the back of the neck while moving up the neck. Experiment, varying the pressure until you can maintain the form of the finger and the note rings throughout, without getting too much resistance as it slides over the frets.

After completing the slide, the third finger needs to jump back to the fourth fret with a minimal pause between the notes. Keep your eye on the destination fret rather than your hand to improve your accuracy.

Your first finger will lead each of the ascending movements in bar three. Keep it held on the E string and pair it with either the second or third fingers, depending on each *dyad* (two-note chord). After using the fourth finger for the high B on beat three, descend into bar four by sliding your third finger. When deciding on fingering for yourself, look for common fingers in adjacent chord shapes to decide how to approach any tricky parts.

In the pickup to the second half of the piece, use fingers one and two. This stretch will prepare you for barring the 10th fret with the fourth finger. Angle your hand so that the knuckles are in vertical alignment, rather than parallel to the strings. This will help the fourth finger reach further along the fretboard.

Even though all the notes are on the highest three strings, plucking with the thumb will produce more tonal separation between the bassline and melody, while requiring less picking dexterity than using all three fingers.

Minuet from Sonata in D – Joseph Haydn

Drop D tuning

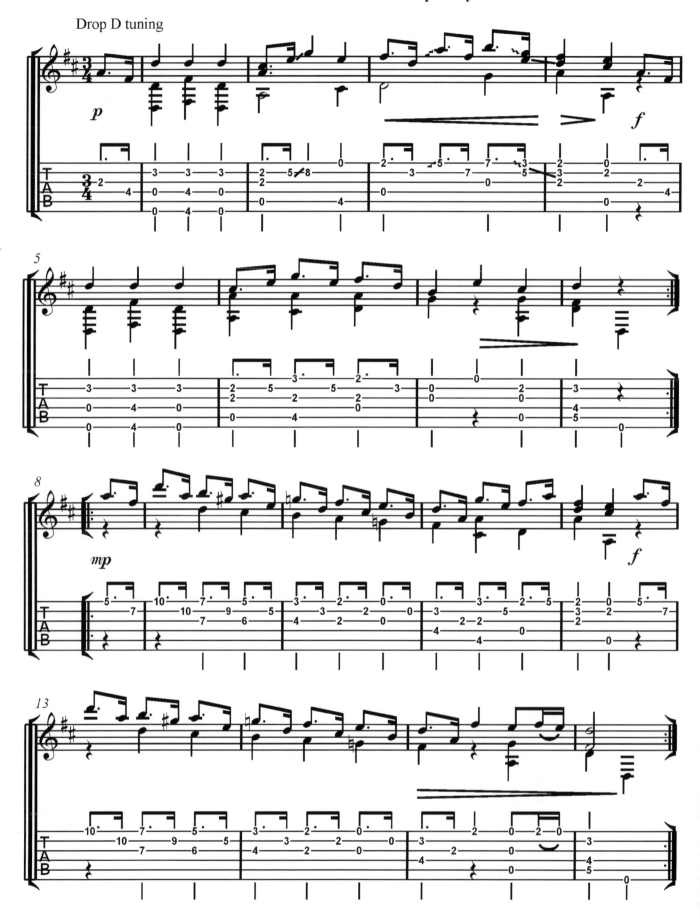

2. Ejercicio No. 9 – José Ferrer

José Ferrer was a Spanish guitarist and composer in the late nineteenth and early twentieth centuries. Born in Girona in 1835, he lived there until his middle age. He then moved to Paris to teach at the conservatoire, before returning to Spain to live in Barcelona for the last fifteen years of his life.

Ferrer composed about a hundred pieces. These were mainly solos or duets for guitars, or flute and guitar. Many of them were published during his lifetime and he gained popularity for his composition and performances, as well as earning an international reputation as a teacher.

This etude is quite similar in style to works produced in the early nineteenth century by composers like Carcassi and Carruli. However, it also illustrates the transition from the Classical to the Romantic period in subtle ways.

For instance, the first four bars outline an Em - Am - B7 - Em progression, using familiar open position chords. Ferrer adds more colour by building the melody using notes not found in these basic chords. In bar two, the effect of the combined chord and melody suggests the movement of Am7 to Am6, and the start of bar 4 suggests an Emadd9.

Be sure to hold down every note for its full duration. The extended harmony in bars two and four will only be apparent if the notes are allowed to ring out over the chords. The downward facing tails indicate which notes should be sustained.

In Classical period compositions, these notes would have been considered dissonances and only used as passing tones between consonant chord tones on each beat. The richer harmony is produced by placing these non-chord tones on strong beats.

Use the thumb and index fingers to pluck the high chords in bars two and four. Although it would be more common to use fingers on the G and B strings, the thumb's softer tone will differentiate the accompaniment from the melody more clearly.

The phrase in bars five to eight is much more Classical in style. You should recognise the use of tenth intervals placed against a repeating open string from many of the pieces in book one.

To prepare for the awkward chord shape in bar fifteen you'll need to change position by sliding your first finger up from the bass note in bar fourteen. Angling the wrist and forearm so the knuckles are in vertical alignment will help you stretch further. Slide your fingers down to the 4th fret on beat 3 while holding the low B down. This harmonic resolution is another example of the Romantic era traits found in the first four bars.

The second half of the piece is built around a crotchet melody in the bass. Make sure each note flows into the next. It will help to hear the melody without the open B string at first. The fingers will need to be arched so they don't accidentally mute the high string. Make sure the last finger knuckles are curled in and the end of the fingertip is in contact with the string.

Lastly, to ensure the notes in bar twenty-six are able to ring properly, use fingers two and three for the notes at the 2nd fret, then slide your second finger up to the 3rd fret before using fingers three and four for the double-stop in bar twenty-seven.

Ejercicio No. 9 – Jose Ferrer

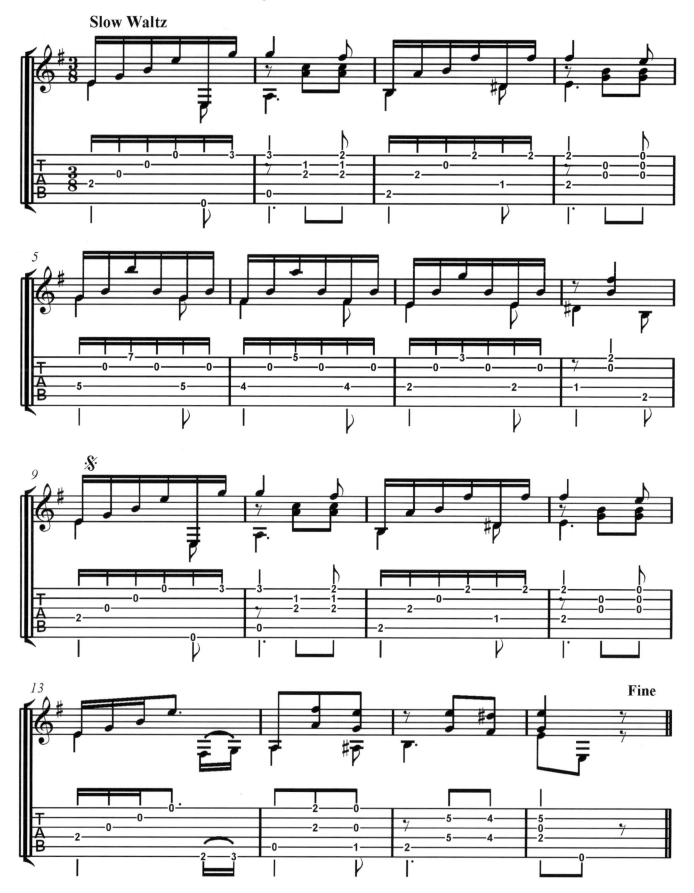

D.S. al Fine

This page is intentionally left blank

3. Study No. 11 Moderato, Op. 31 – Fernando Sor

Fernando Sor's studies for guitar continue to be very popular among classical guitarists, two hundred years after their composition. The famous guitarist and teacher Andrés Segovia published a set of twenty studies by Sor in 1945, which helped to revitalise Sor's legacy and keep his music central to the modern guitarist's development.

Volume one covered several pieces by Sor including the perennial *Study No. 22 in B Minor*, but here we have a less well-known study from his *Op. 31* collection.

There's plenty of expressive dynamic changes in *Study No. 11*, and the 6/8 rhythm gives it a dance-like character. The feel is very similar to Carcassi's *Diversion No. 6* (piece number 14 in this book).

Dynamics refer to volume. They range from **p** (*piano* – soft) to **f** (*forte* – loud). Between these lie **mp** (*mezzo piano* – moderately soft) and **mf** (*mezzo forte* – moderately loud). A repeating letter indicates an extreme of range. E.g. **pp** would mean very quietly.

Several familiar open chord shapes are smuggled through as single notes. Spotting the chords on which the piece is built will help you finger it correctly and memorise it more easily. The first phrase is based around F, C and Bb barre chords.

The small notes, as in bar seven, are called *acciaccaturas* (or "grace notes" in jazz or pop parlance). They don't have their own rhythmic value, so are not included in counting the length of the bar. Instead they should be played as quickly as possible, leading into the next full-length note.

The rhythm of bar seven might be tricky at first. If so, play the top line without the chords to first master the tune and the acciaccatura. Work on the second half of the bar in isolation to get the sequence of fingers flowing smoothly. As always, listen to the audio examples to clarify the rhythm.

The same idea crops up twice in the B section. The pull-off from the third fret should be executed with the fourth finger, while the third holds down the bass note for the full bar. Checking in the notation for which notes hang down from the dots is a good indicator as to whether they should be held down or not.

Bars fourteen and fifteen are the dramatic climax. Dig in harder with the picking hand and slow down to give a sense of weight to these notes. Listen to the audio to hear how I lean on the Bb Minor and Bb Major chords in bar fifteen to make the most of the striking harmonic change. Use a quick downward pull-off.

The musical release in the following bar should return to an even tempo until it comes to rest on F Major in bar seventeen. Here the high A is sustained while the descending bassline is marked with staccato dots, meaning they should be short and punchy.

Position the first finger carefully at the start of bar nineteen to prepare for the ensuing barre with minimal readjustment.

Finally, the closing section from bar twenty-one onwards uses a call and response between high double-stops and low chord/bassline phrases. Pay attention to the dynamics marks to make this convincing and memorable.

The last four F chords should diminish gradually. The musical drama has already been resolved and we are just settling down to gradually land on the final root note.

Op. 31, Study No. 11 Moderato – Fernando Sor

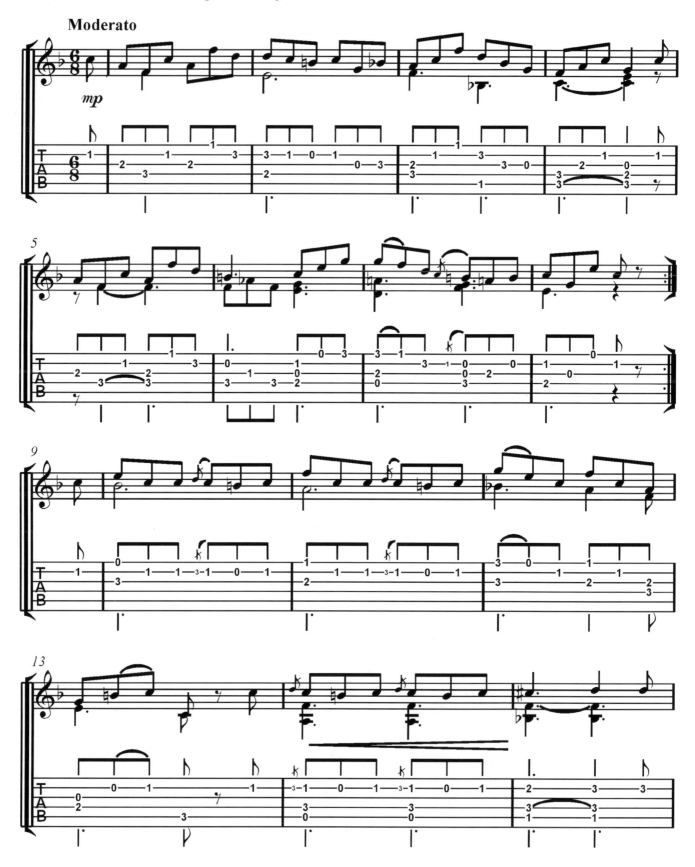

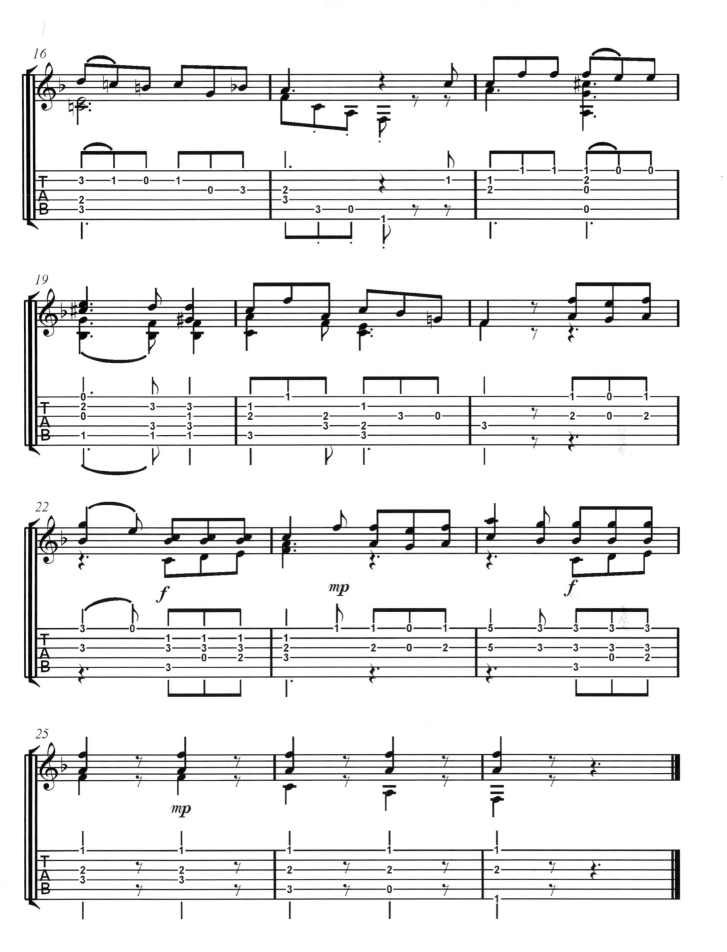

This page is intentionally left blank

4. Waltz in D, Op. 7, No. 2 – Dionisio Aguado

Our next composer is the Spanish classical guitarist Dionisio Aguado (1784-1849). Aguado was born in Madrid and upon moving to Paris became friends with Fernando Sor. Over his lifetime Aguado had sixteen published works which vary greatly in length and difficulty. In addition, his early method book is still in print today.

In the early nineteenth century guitars had shorter scale lengths. Unfortunately, this makes the wide stretches contained in pieces from this period much more challenging to play on a modern guitar.

The use of a grace note (*acciaccatura*) and a demi-semiquaver makes bar one look rhythmically complex, but listen carefully to the audio and copy the phrasing. Play the first bar slowly enough so that you can tap your foot on each of the three quavers in the bar. Matching the second A note to the second foot tap will keep the phrasing in check. The opening motif is varied several times throughout the piece, so getting comfortable with bar one will pay dividends later.

The tune moves around the fretboard and the bigger shifts will take isolated practice to master. The first shift is from the 10th fret with the fourth finger, down to the 3rd fret with the first finger. Often there are easier places these notes can be played, but the way I've notated the piece allows chord tones to ring together as much as possible.

Keep each finger held down as you build up the D Major chord (using the C shape) in bar two. In the following two bars, don't use your first finger for the A Major chord, but add it for the third shape to lead into bar four on the E string. The D Major chord in bar four should use your first, second and third fingers, leaving the fourth free to start the recurring melodic motif.

The chromatic passing tone in bar fifteen is of particular interest. As well as allowing the melody line to move smoothly between two chords, it also has a harmonic role. Notice how the F natural adds colour to the piece. It implies a chord progression of D Major to D Minor to A Major. The D Minor chord doesn't belong in this key, but is a common substitution in many styles of music. Commit this sound to memory and you'll start recognising it in lots of pieces of all styles.

Bars twenty-one and twenty-two feature two position shifts in quick succession. Follow the fingerings I've written for the best results. The fretting hand will have to stretch and shrink as it moves down the fretboard in a "crab-walk" fashion.

Lastly, remember that this is a waltz, so every phrase should have a strong, consistent rhythmic pulse, even if you pause expressively at the end of phrases – most of which last for eight bars.

Waltz in D, Op. 7, No. 2 – Dionisio Aguado

D.C. al Fine

This page is intentionally left blank

5. Bagatelle No. 2, Op. 4 - Heinrich Marschner

Although less well remembered than his contemporaries (Beethoven, Wagner and Schumann), Heinrich Marschner was a master of German opera and much adored during his lifetime. He also wrote songs and instrumental chamber music. This bagatelle from Marschner is rather brief at a modest sixteen bars (excluding repeats), but he packs a lot in.

The frequent changes between different plucking patterns can be confusing at first. There are double-stop melodies, alternating thumb/claw patterns, four-note chords and rolling arpeggios to tackle. Once all of the sections have been digested separately, the challenge is to make them flow as a cohesive piece of music.

A great aid to developing your performance is to record yourself playing. Listening back to yourself will allow you to be more objective about your playing and hear it from an audience's perspective. Listen out for unintended changes in dynamics or tempo. To make the sections flow together there shouldn't be a discernible change between the different techniques, unless the music specifically calls for it.

The A section has lots of familiar chord shapes such as D, G and A, but we need some alternative fingerings to navigate through those changes while holding the bass notes down. The G Major chord in bar one should be played with the third finger on the low root note, freeing up the remaining fingers for the high double-stops. This eases the change to E7 on beat 4. Swap from the third finger on the low G, to first, second and fourth fingers for the E7.

Keep the second finger held down for the change from E7 to A in bar two. The third finger on the G string is then common to the next chord.

Another such example occurs in bar six where the A Major chord is played differently. The D string isn't needed, so just use fingers one and two for the two fretted notes.

Arguably the most technically demanding section is the rapid-fire chord changes in bar eleven. Eight chord shapes in one bar! The first four are the same as those in bars one and two, so the fingering instructions above will help you. A sudden shift is needed to reach the fifth chord, however, then the fingerings I've added to the notation should see you home and dry.

Thankfully, the tempo is quite slow, but there should be minimal space between each chord. Once you've memorised each chord shape, play the whole bar slowly, repeating it every day. Eventually the sequence will become second nature and it will feel like one continuous motion.

Bars twelve and thirteen are mostly recycling material already used in the A section.

Watch out for the triplets at the end of the piece. The overall beat should remain constant throughout, but instead of counting 1 & 2 & etc., each beat is subdivided: 1 & a, 2 & a.

For the first three shapes, lead with the fourth finger on the high E string.

The *sfz* symbol means *sforzando*. Much like the accent arrow >, it calls for a sudden loud attack. That means the chord at the end of beat four should be loudly strummed, despite the general dynamic marking of *piano* marked in bar twelve.

Bagatelle No. 2, Op. 4 - Heinrich Marschner

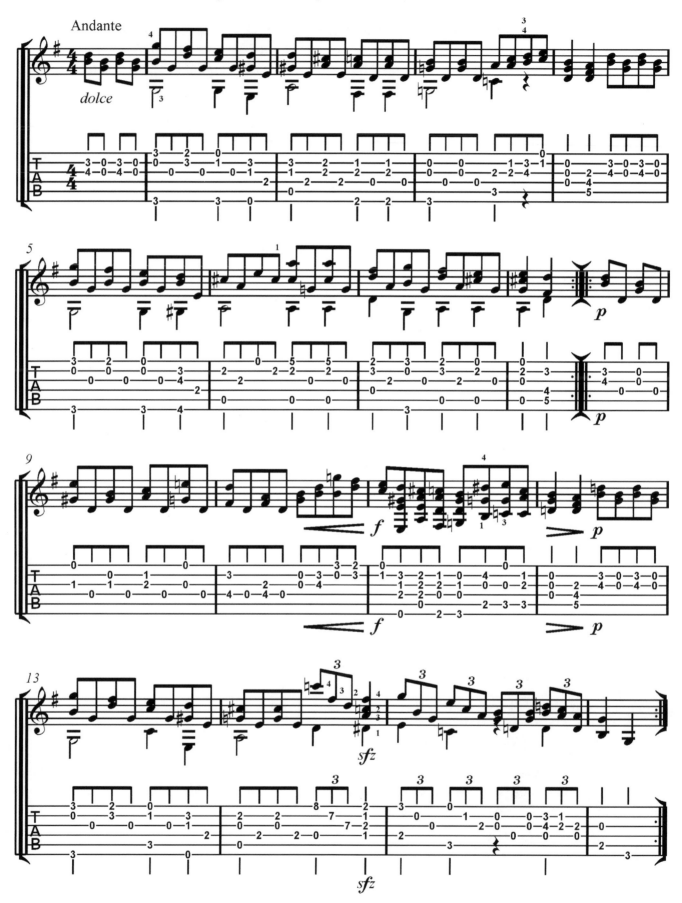

6. ¡Adelita! – Francisco Tárrega

Back to Espania now for a short Tárrega piece. Adelita is based on a *mazurka* (see below). Interpreting dance forms and how they became a part of classical music was addressed in volume one. This beautiful example shows how the character of a dance can be translated into a performance piece.

The mazurka was originally a Polish dance that spread throughout European culture. It's always in 3/4 time signature and has a pronounced "1 & 2, 3" count with the emphasis on beat 2 or 3. The dance should be at a lively speed and the overall effect is something of a march combined with a waltz. The bounce of the triple time is kept in check by the strict rhythmic phrasing.

Chopin wrote many mazurkas for the piano and, being Polish, he would have been very familiar with the authentic feel. It's interesting to consider that we're hearing this form through the ears of Tárrega. His Spanish influence can be detected if you compare performances of the work by both composers. Listen to Tárrega's *Mazurka in G Major* and note any rhythmic similarities. His languid Spanish interpretation is still present, but the composition is more complex with elaborate embellishments throughout.

Adelita uses legato techniques to make the melodic phrases feel relaxed. There are several long slides and many hammer-ons and pull-offs.

Aguado's *Waltz* and *Sor's Study No. 11* featured acciaccaturas, but here two are used in quick succession in bar four. Listen carefully to the audio to hear how the rhythm pauses over the bar line to allow space for this embellishment before the full length notes are placed on beat one.

Bar four also features our first slide. Most players pause after the initial flourish, then speed up again on the remaining five notes which flow into beat 1 of the next bar. The 7th fret should be played with the fourth finger, which is then held down and slid up to the 12th fret.

If the stretch between the 3rd and 7th frets proves uncomfortable, lower your thumb on the back of the neck. Take regular rests and keep your hand as relaxed as possible to avoid any strain.

The structure of the piece is AABA. The A section is in the sombre key of E Minor, while the B section provides a dramatic contrast. Notice how the mood brightens when we transition to bar nine. Such colourful use of harmony is characteristic of the Romantic period. The liberal juxtaposition of keys was a radical break from the Classical style where harmonic shifts would be made by logical developments through cadences and closely related keys. Changing from a major key to a minor key on the same root note (in this case E) is known as a *parallel modulation*.

The musical climax of the piece occurs in bars ten and eleven. To prepare for the slide up to the 12th fret, barre the D shape chord at the 4th fret with the first finger. Both sets of acciaccaturas should be played with the third and fourth fingers. This leaves the first and second fingers free to hold down the bass notes.

There is much expression to be drawn out of bar thirteen, so after getting confident with the notes, work on following the dynamic markings. *Molto ten* is short for *tenuto*, which means the notes should be held longer. Imagine that each of the notes are suddenly "heavier" and this will help the phrase to drag appropriately.

¡Adelita! – Francisco Tárrega

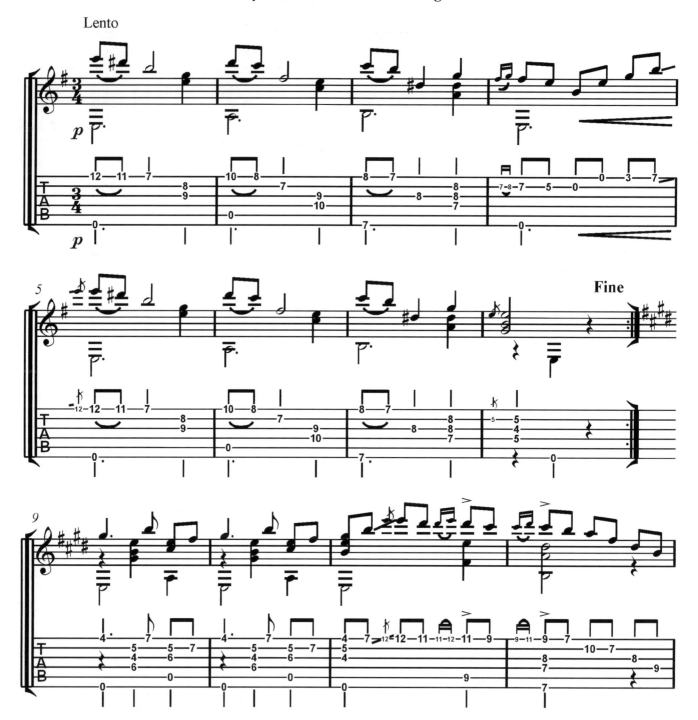

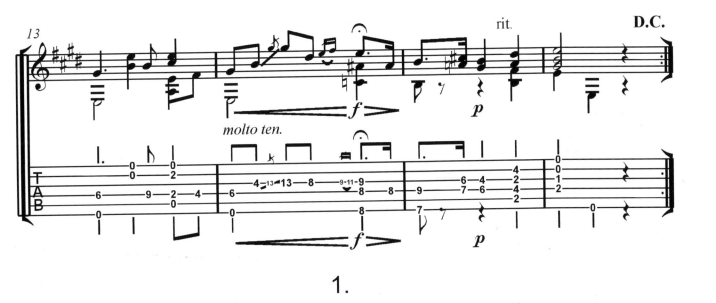

1.

This page is intentionally left blank

7. Waltz in E Major – Matteo Carcassi

We step back in time from Tárrega to look at a piece by Carcassi. This waltz in E Major is the first piece from his *Op. 16* collection of solo pieces entitled *Diversions*.

This waltz highlights the importance of emphasising different beats to produce a particular feel. The rhythm of the opening bars looks very similar to Tárrega's *Mazurka*, but to differentiate the waltz from the mazurka, adopt a less rigid feel and accent both beats 2 and 3 to get a 1 **2 3**, 1 **2 3** feel.

This piece uses Open E tuning. "Open tuning" means the strings are tuned to a common open chord shape. In Open E, the strings are tuned to an E chord, from low to high: E, B, E, G#, B, E. Other common tunings in acoustic guitar music are Open D and Open G.

When playing in Open E, the D and A strings need to be tuned up an entire tone so you might consider restringing them with lighter gauge strings – especially if you're playing these pieces on a steel strung acoustic with high tension strings. Alternatively, you could detune every string a tone and then tune to Open E to reduce stress on the guitar neck. You can play the notation/tab as normal, but the piece will now sound like it's in the key of D Major.

In bars one and two the use of open strings may seem easy, but the melody will be blurred if you don't mute the high E string as you play the B after it. The best way to achieve this is to bring your picking hand fingers back down onto the strings afterwards. Practise bringing **a** back on to the E string just as **m** plucks the B string, so that there is a seamless transition between the two, with no overlap.

Your hand should remain in the fourth position for the first section, except for bar three when a position shift back to the first fret is needed to play the ascending chromatic scale. Be prepared to take this bar very slowly to get the coordination between all four fretting hand fingers.

The B section combines two interesting techniques. Bar nine moves chord fragments along the top two strings. Although one note is played at a time, each beat is a chord and the notes should be held down together. Use the first finger on the E string throughout and alternate second and third fingers on the B string, depending on the chord shape.

These chord fragment sequences are contrasted with some natural harmonics. Because of the altered tuning, these harmonics form beautiful, delicate major chords. You'll need to pay close attention to the changes in hand position from the fretted notes at the start of each bar to laying a finger flat across the strings for the harmonics. Remember to gently touch the strings directly over the fret wire for good, clear harmonics and then remove your finger once they have sounded to avoid muting them prematurely.

Bar seventeen to the end shouldn't pose any problems, but remember to observe the sudden change in dynamics from *f* to *pp*.

Waltz in E major – Matteo Carcassi

Open E major tuning

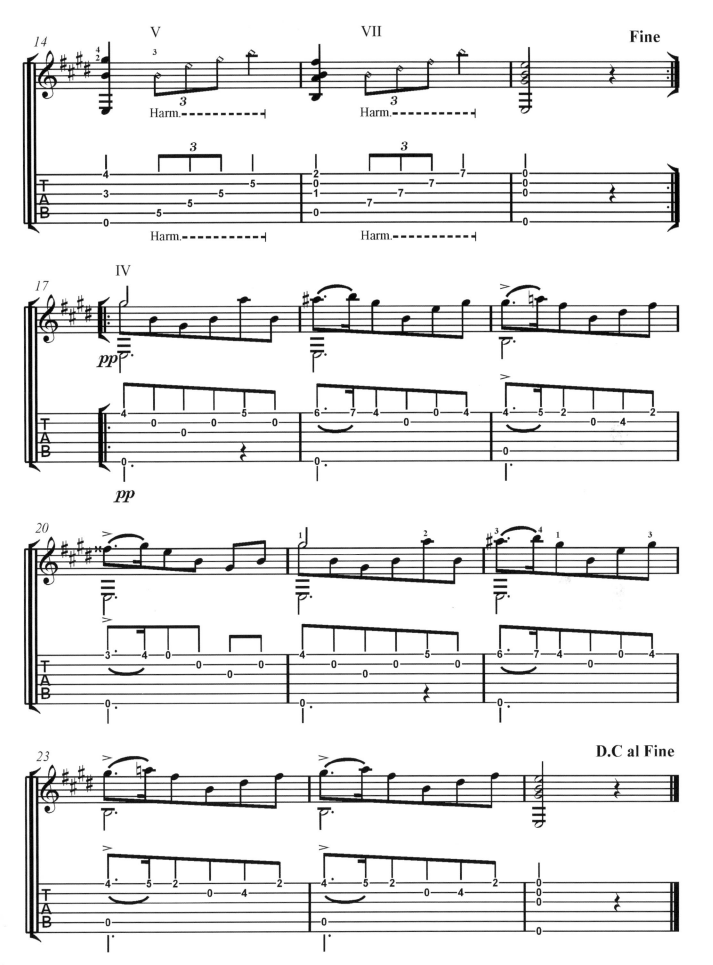

This page is intentionally left blank

8. Pavane – Gaspar Sanz

Gaspar Sanz (1640-1710) was a Spanish composer, theologian and priest in the early Baroque period. His main instrument was the organ, but while travelling to Italy in order to continue his education he took up the guitar and it's that for which he's now remembered.

Like other composers we've studied, Sanz became a noted guitar teacher upon his return to Spain, even teaching the King's son. He published three volumes of pedagogical pieces entitled *Instrucción de Música Sobre la Guitarra Española* in 1674, 75 and 97.

The original manuscripts are freely available online and I recommend looking them up for an interesting glimpse into music history. There are some amusingly awkward chord "diagrams" depicting a disembodied hand and, more interestingly, the pieces are written in an archaic form of tablature. Upon first glance, it looks very familiar: numbers on lines, divided into bars with rhythmic values floating above the tab staff. However, if you try to play from this tab, it sounds dreadful!

The reason is that the layout of the strings on the page is reversed. This makes some sense, as beginners are often confused by the down-is-up geography of guitar parlance. Today, we read tab with the high pitch on the top line. My theory is that the "flip" occurred around the time when conventional notation became dominant throughout Europe and guitarists began to use both systems.

Most crucially, there are only five lines. The Baroque guitar had only five strings, which were sometimes paired, similar to a 12-string guitar or mandolin. This instrument represented a transitional phase as the renaissance era lute slowly evolved into the modern guitar. Consequently, we hardly need to touch our low E string in this piece. That said, in bars eleven and twelve, I decided to add some extra "oomph" by writing in a low G, F and E, giving some gravity to the end of that phrase.

In *Pavane* there are plenty of solo scale runs that build up to chords, as well as sections of bassline played across sustained higher notes. Careful fingering choices are needed to avoid cutting notes short. In bar one use fingers one and three for the A Minor chord, which is held down over the moving bassline. In bar two, the second finger can sustain the root note throughout, while the fourth and first fingers play the melody.

Bars eight and nine will need special attention to get the melody to flow seamlessly. Practise the single note line first without the bass note to get the sound in your mind. Singing it out loud will help. Notice how the melody arrives on beat three of bar nine, just as the bassline starts its build-up into bar ten. This overlapping of melodic parts gives a hint of the "counterpoint" style of Bach (I covered Bach's *Bourrée* in book one). It is also known as "dovetailing" parts.

In bars twenty-six and twenty-seven you must change position before each bass note, so it can be held over the quick three-note bursts. Use hammer-ons to make them smooth and fast. If you're not comfortable with hammer-ons and pull-offs, then picking with alternating fingers will help.

The *pavane* was an Italian processional dance, popular across Europe in the sixteenth and seventeenth centuries, so in terms of feel aim for a proud, regal affectation by placing emphasis on the first and third beats throughout.

Pavana – Gaspar Sanz

33

This page is intentionally left blank

9. She Moved Through the Fair – Traditional

Here's a less well-known piece from the British folk music canon. This tune was first collected from Ireland and – as with so much of the folk tradition – now exists in many versions with different titles in other regions. The lyrics have a much more traceable route back to the poet Padraic Colum, who expanded on a verse of traditional words and set them to the tune.

This arrangement starts with a stark rendition of the main tune before embarking on a series of variations that use drone notes underneath moving chords, big block chords, and some instances of counter melody.

Playing a solo melody calls for subtle, expressive techniques to give it personality. Add some vibrato to the longer notes and imagine how a singer would naturally sing louder as the notes go higher. Start each phrase quietly so you will be able to pluck harder as you ascend, giving the melody more character to retain listener interest.

Make sure the A notes at the 5th fret in bar three are fretted with the fourth finger, as this will leave the remaining fingers free to smoothly transition into the following chord. The upward arrows indicate to strum the chord slowly, so each note can be heard. This gives emphasis to the top notes which form the melody.

Consider taking the opposite approach to dynamics in bars four and five. As the melody moves back down to the D, gradually soften your attack to bring the phrase to a rest.

Each melody note in the next section is harmonised with a new chord. Seeing the shapes as part of common major and minor barre chords will help you identify each one and make learning and understanding the music easier. The D string is sustained throughout. This is known as a *pedal tone*. The effect creates a subtle tension between the static bassline and moving chords.

Bar seventeen has a short section of countermelody. The main tune ascends slowly, while the faster moving second tune wends its way downwards. Producing both notes consistently will take careful practise to ensure your technique is spot on, especially the G/F# pair on beat four.

The chord shapes start to get more demanding from bar twenty-one onwards. They are more jazz-influenced and chromatic compared to the first half of the piece and there are no open strings to take up the slack. The picking should be a regular pattern of **p** alternating with **i**, **m** and **a** in a claw motion.

To close the piece, we have one last chord-based phrase. As with the preceding bars we have four chords, one per beat. The bass notes are placed ahead of the rest of the chord to add a sense of movement to the ending.

She Moved Through the Fair – Traditional

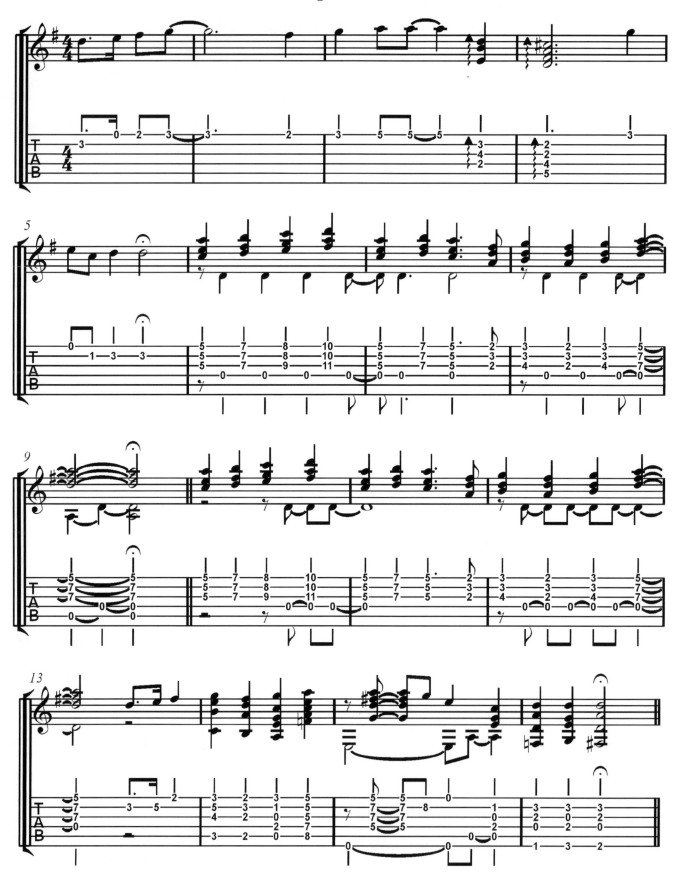

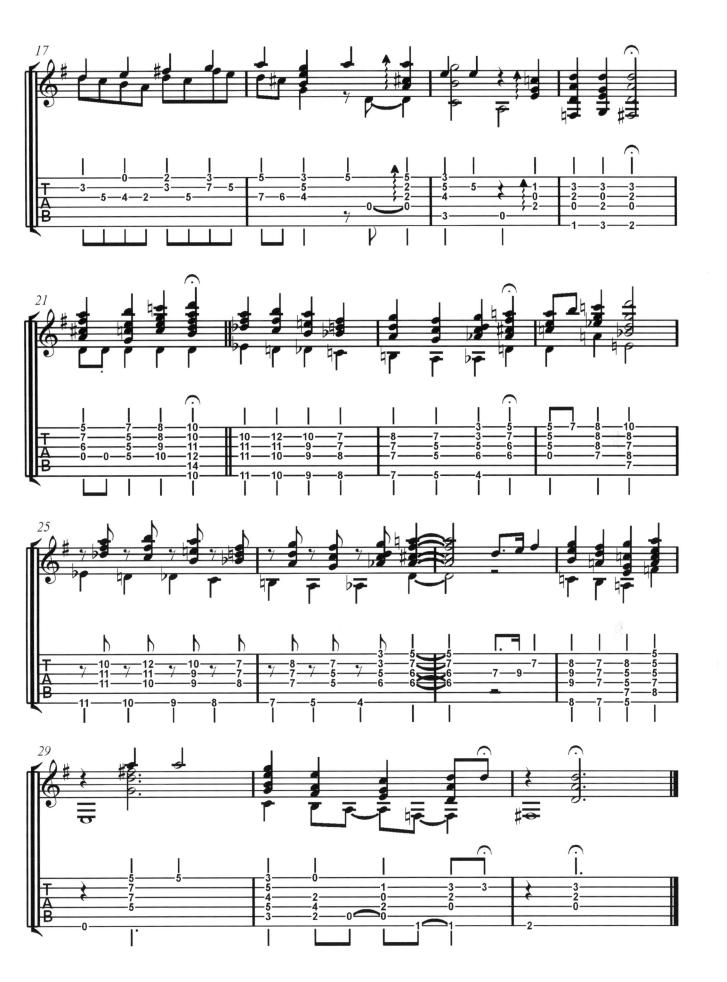

This page is intentionally left blank

10. Newport Fair – Rob Thorpe

Keeping with the folk theme, I wrote this piece to explore solo guitar accompaniment ideas. It draws inspiration from the great fingerstyle players of the 1960s folk revival, such as Bert Jansch, Davy Graham, Jackson C. Frank, and Richard Thompson.

The title is, of course, a reference to various British ballads that feature fairs, such as Brigg Fair and Scarborough Fair. The famed Newport Folk Festival in Rhode Island began in 1959 and introduced many now legendary folk artists, like Bob Dylan and Joan Baez, to a young American audience.

You'll find a mixture of techniques here, including an alternating bassline, legato embellishments, banjo rolls, drone notes in chords, and simultaneous melody and bassline combinations (known as Travis Picking in country guitar).

Make sure that the basic thumb pattern in the introduction is stable and effortless before you move on, as it is the foundation for everything that follows.

The next four bars feature a simpler melody than the main tune, but make sure you are confident with each section before moving on and you will make faster progress in the long run.

Keep things simple and practise playing all four bass notes on one string. Then play the full picking pattern on open strings before adding the chord shapes. If coordinating your picking hand proves difficult, then analyse the rhythm and identify if the melody notes fall on the bass notes or between them. Count it out slowly. Introduce notes one by one at first. Work from the bassline up. Keeping this even is your highest priority in this style.

The rhythm is identical in each bar. Once you have learnt the first two bars, you will be able to play the third and fourth bars with only a small adjustment to change strings.

Once you start to tackle the more intricate main tune, be sure to break it down into small chunks – even as short as one beat. Repeating these short phrases in time with steady bass notes will train your picking hand for any combination of thumb and fingers.

Carefully arch your fingers for the contrasting rolling chords near the end, so that the open E and B strings aren't accidentally muted. Many interesting new chords can be found by combining open strings with fragments of open chord shapes and moving them up the neck. Don't worry about the names of these chords, just enjoy their individual colours.

The picking pattern is the difficult bit here, as the tempo is quite quick. I choose to pick it using **p i p m** which requires the least finger independence. The more classical approach of **p m i a** is another option that gives a brighter tone.

Experiment on your own by moving fragments of chords up the neck in this fashion and see what you come up!

Newport Fair – Rob Thorpe

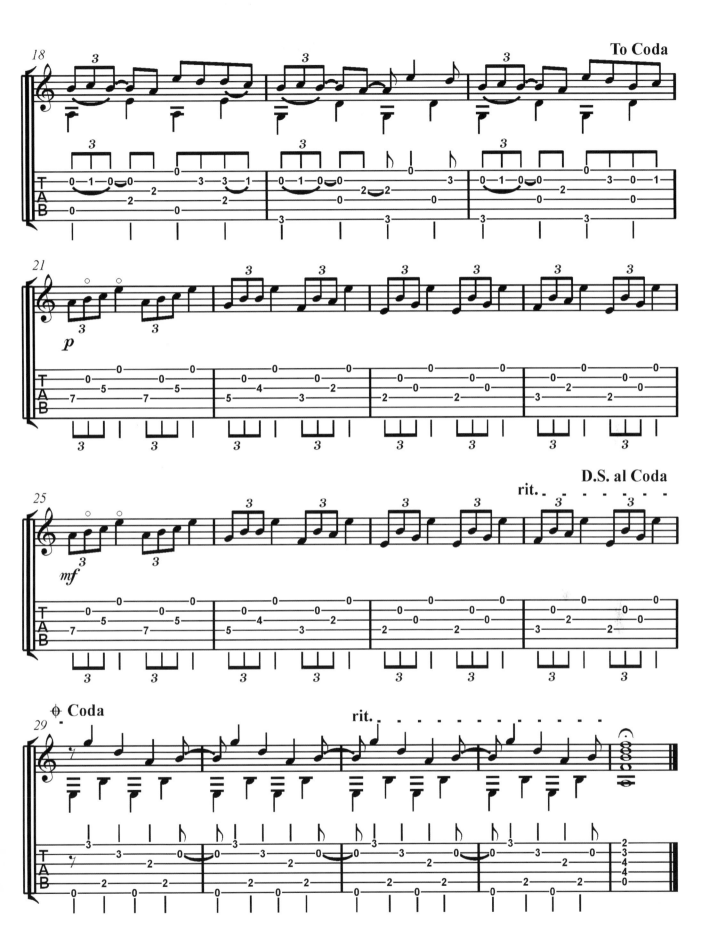

This page is intentionally left blank

11. Minuet in C from Sonata Op. 29 – Anton Diabelli

Continuing our exploration of different dance forms in 3/4 time, which so far has included the mazurka and waltz, we now have a minuet. It comes from Diabelli's larger *Sonata in C* for solo guitar, but is perfect to perform as a standalone single movement.

The minuet is characterised by the pickup beats into bars one, nine and onwards. There should also be a strong first beat in every bar, in contrast to the other two dances which emphasised beats 2 and 3.

Keep your first finger held down on the high C throughout the first four bars while your remaining fingers tackle the ascending bassline. Keep your thumb low on the back of the neck if you struggle to arch the fingers enough to avoid muting the high note.

The descending melody in bar five is a tricky moment in the piece. Developing the flexibility to stretch from the 1st to 5th fret may seem daunting, but will come with regular practice. Gently work on your fretting hand span every day after warming up.

An effective exercise would be to move the three notes much higher on the fretboard where the spacing is closer, and practise these pull-offs. When the stretch from, say, the 8th to 12th fret feels comfortable, work your way down towards the first position, taking several weeks to do so if necessary.

The slides in bars thirty-five and thirty-nine facilitate the position shifts and also add some tonal variety. Use your fourth finger in bar thirty-five, so the F bass note can be held down for its full duration. Slide the fourth finger up to the 5th fret, keeping enough pressure to sustain the note.

A common mistake is to rush hammer-ons, pull-offs and slides, and not give the starting note its full rhythmic value. Count evenly through these bars at first to ensure you're allowing the G at the 3rd fret to ring long enough, before sliding up quickly for beat one. Tapping your foot can help you to avoid rushing.

In bar thirty-nine, use your fourth finger again to prepare for the next bar, where you'll use your third finger for the bass note on beat 1.

The form of the piece is that each section should be played with repeats in order, before returning to the top and starting again, then continuing to the *Fine* sign. After the D.C. the first two sections should be played again without their individual repeats.

I've added several dynamic marks to help you get more contrast out of the different sections. This will add more drama to the performance. Pieces from the Baroque period don't often prescribe dynamics or tempo, as the performers were intended to interpret these themselves.

Minuet in C from Sonata Op. 29 – Anton Diabelli

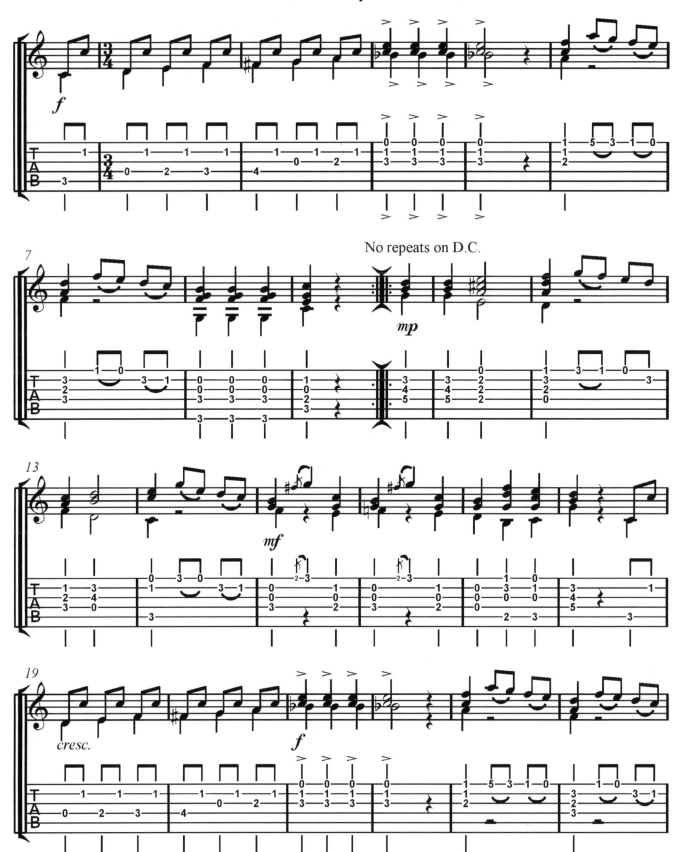

No repeats on D.C.

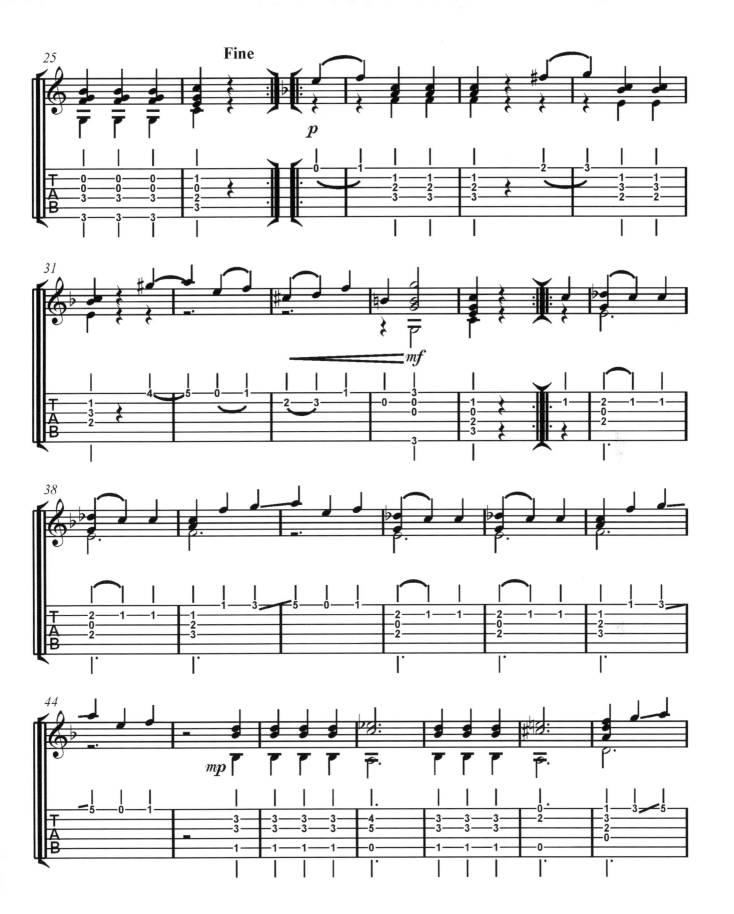

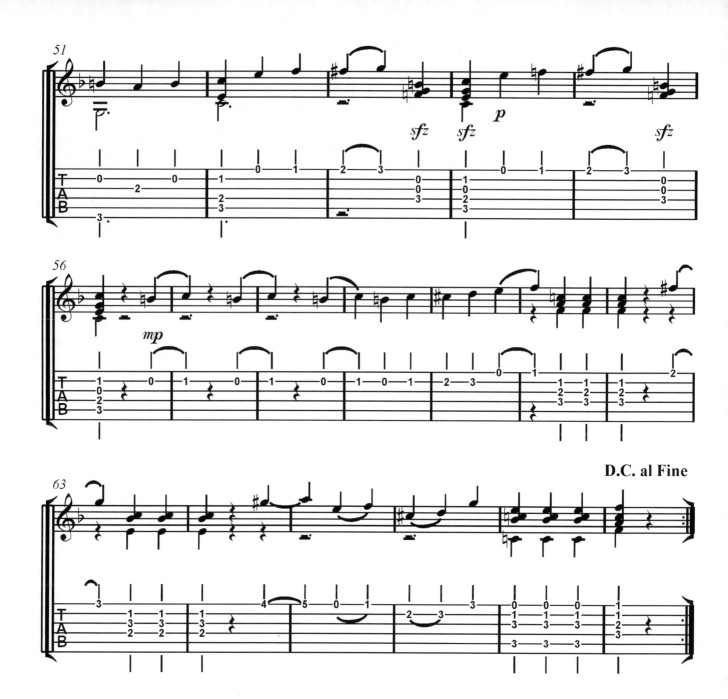

D.C. al Fine

12. Prelude No. 1 – Francisco Tárrega

The term "prelude" doesn't indicate a particular form or rhythmic template, unlike the various dances we've looked at. As the name suggests, a prelude was usually the introduction to a larger suite of music, as in Bach's famous "cello suites". By the Romantic era, however, the prelude could also be a free-standing piece, usually of fairly short duration. Chopin's piano preludes are amongst the most famous and we'll look at one of those later.

This prelude by Tárrega makes use of the same Drop D tuning as Haydn's minuet – the first piece we looked at. The low E string is dropped a tone to D to enhance the bass register.

Straight off the bat there are some quick position shifts to master. Play the first two notes with your second and fourth fingers to reach the second bass note smoothly. Practise changing from playing the 8th fret with the second finger, to placing the fourth finger at the 6th fret and playing the bass note with the first finger. Memorise how far your hand needs to move and concentrate on the bass note. This will help you to be more consistent.

Bar five has the first of several sliding grace notes. Listen carefully to the audio to hear what it should sound like. Try singing what you're going to play. If you can accurately sing what you're hearing, it will be easier to train your hands to repeat it. Slide the A up to C, slightly ahead of when you should pick it, and then once you arrive at C, re-pick it to get the last quaver of the bar.

There are several instances in this piece where you'll need to barre more strings than are played in order to prepare for the following notes. The first example of this comes in bar five where the initial F chord should barre the top two strings to give a smooth transition to the second note. A less obvious occurrence is in bar seven. Barre across the 8th fret for the whole bar, so there isn't an awkward gap before beat two.

Break the long descending melody starting in bar thirteen into small chunks to ensure each chord shape is internalised. The second chord in bar fourteen is particularly tricky. Use your third, then first fingers for the melody, with the second and fourth holding down the other chord tones. Start with just the melody then add the A note with your second finger. Finally, make the wide stretch to add the low F# at the fourth fret.

Thankfully, this long section of chord shapes is repeated identically later in the piece. Put the time in to nail it once and you'll have cracked a sizeable chunk of the whole piece.

There is one last gargantuan position shift to drill in bar twenty-two: a leap from the 11th fret down to the 3rd! Furthermore, it needs to be done with the pinkie, so that it flows between the chord shapes that bookend it. Take the pressure off the string as you move, so there isn't an audible *glissando* (slide). There will be a silence between the notes, but with practice and speed this will gradually be minimised. Alternatively, you could always take the creative decision to make an audible gliss by keeping the pressure on. Just watch out for accidentally muting the G string which should ring throughout.

Prelude No. 1 – Francisco Tárrega

Drop D tuning

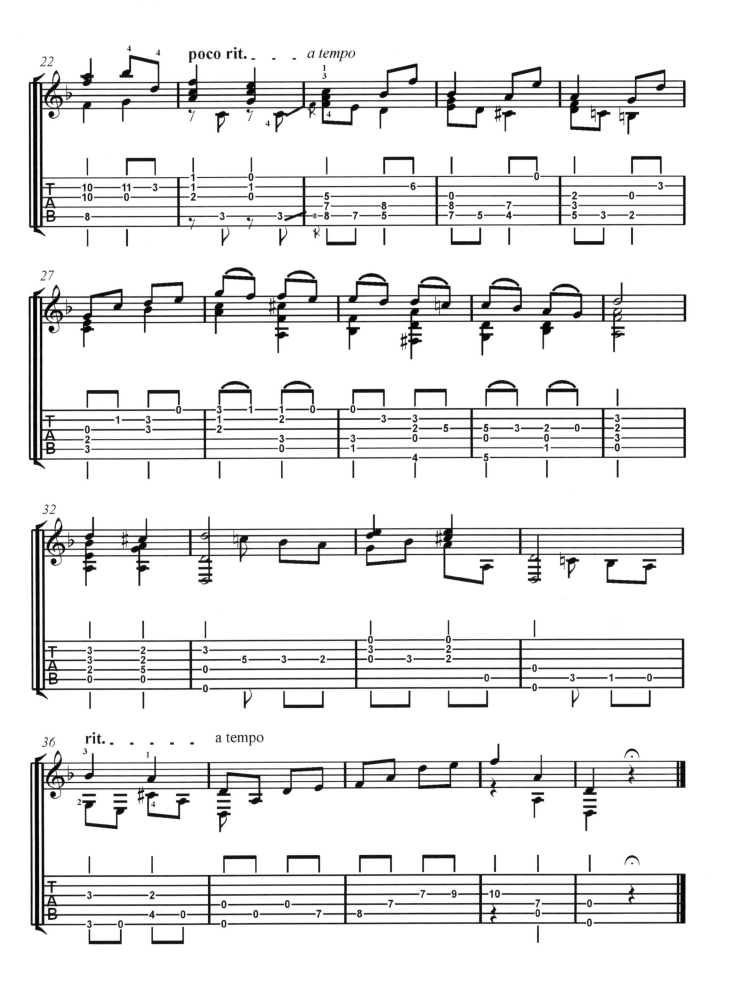

This page is intentionally left blank

13. Cromarty – Rob Thorpe

Here's another composition of mine. It has a consistent picking pattern that will help you develop your speed, while your fretting hand moves through a series of different chord progressions.

We saw a similar use of tenth intervals in Carulli's *Andantino* and Carcassi's *French Dance* in the first volume, but the use of multiple open strings here creates a richer drone effect that combines with the fretting notes to create colourful, unpredictable chords.

You can hear similar chordal ideas in modern acoustic guitar music like that of Michael Hedges, Newton Faulkner and David Mead.

However, this repetitive motif can soon get boring for the listener, so we bring it to life with some dynamics.

It is natural to change speed as we change volume and while some change of speed is expressive, it is important to practise evenly, so that speed and dynamics can be controlled independently. Use a metronome to help you maintain an even tempo as you practise changing volume.

The piece is composed in three sections. The first two feature the fast picking pattern with a key change in the B section which shifts the mood. Section C provides a stark contrast by dropping the tempo and playing spacious quavers.

The chords should be held for their full length. The pauses, or *fermatas,* marked over the last note allow for space between the chords (for your own dramatic interpretation). The use of space heightens the contrast between this section and the very rigid tempo of the rest of the piece.

After section C, the piece returns to the start for another run through A and B, before taking the Coda sign to the end, with a one bar restatement of the C motif.

When trying to increase your playing speed, it is easy to tense up, but this will hinder your progress and potentially cause injury. A good tip to developing speed is to practise short bursts of faster speeds, interspersed with longer periods of slow repetition. Try accelerating for about 5 seconds, then returning to a completely relaxed speed for 20 seconds. Repeat this in cycles and stop if any tension builds up.

Cromarty – Rob Thorpe

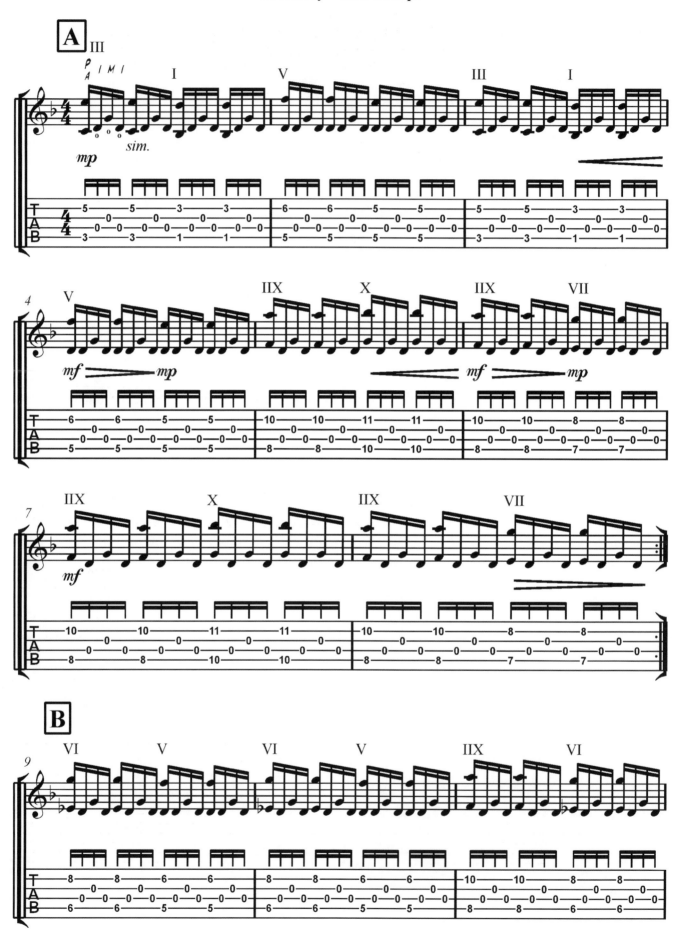

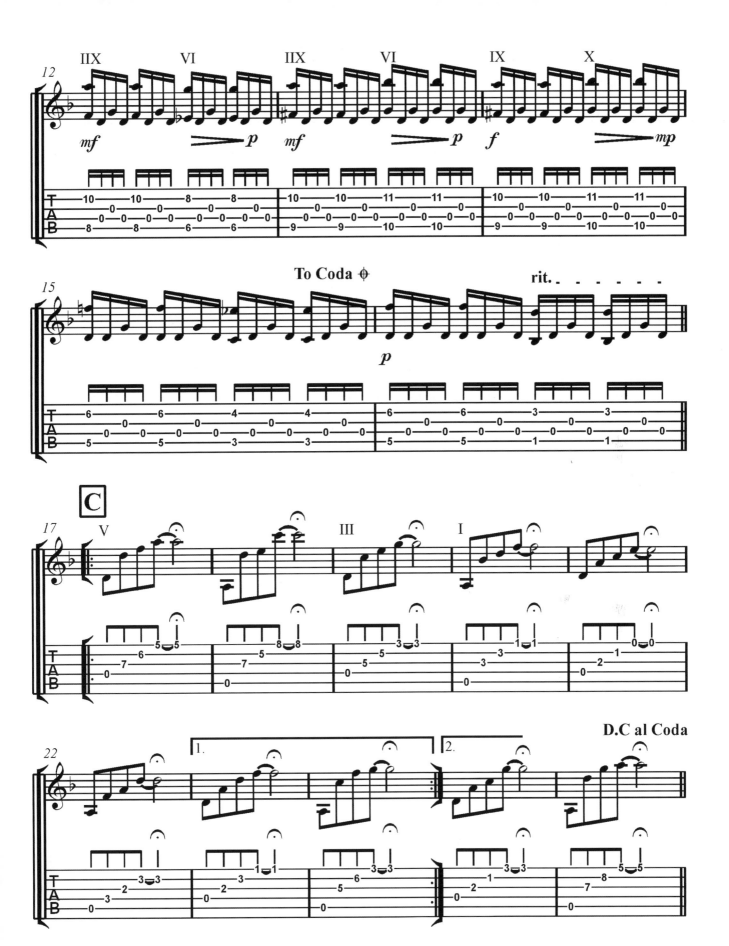

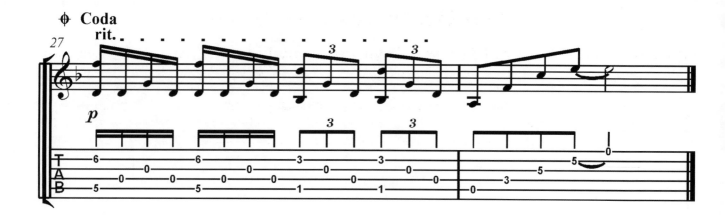

14. Diversions Op. 16, No. 6 – Matteo Carcassi

Now we have another instalment from Carcassi's *Divertissements*. This one is marked as *grazioso*, which translates as "graceful" or "pretty". It should be worked up to a moderate tempo.

I suggest you only tackle this piece after you've become confident with his *Opus 10, no. 1* and have been playing that for a while. It uses several of the same techniques, including harmonics, legato and multiple position shifts, but deploys them in a more complex way involving quicker changes. There are also some big barre chords spanning all six strings.

This piece uses the same Open E tuning as piece No.7, Carcassi's *Waltz in E Major*, so your guitar should be tuned to E, B, E, G#, B, E.

By now, you should have the confidence and understanding to tackle much of this piece using the approaches already addressed.

Use your middle finger to fret the harmonics in bar five. If you've always used your first finger for them this may take a little readjustment, but it means you're in the correct position to fret the melody in the next bar that starts at the 4th fret. Here we also have our first difficult position shift: the F# at the 7th fret will be played with the fourth finger, after which you must jump to the 3rd fret with the first finger to begin the next phrase.

The B section concludes with a hammer-on motif moving up the length of the string. This shouldn't prove too difficult as long as you keep a careful eye on the next fret. The open string sounding between each hammer-on gives you time to shift position. Use your first and second fingers throughout. Once you can play this movement up to tempo, add some dynamics. The harmonics should start at *p*, but this climax should be much louder since it's marked *f*.

At bar eleven we have our first big barre. Unfortunately, there is no hiding in a situation like this if a guitarist's barres aren't up to scratch, but with regular practice all six strings will be consistently clean and the hand will be relaxed. To make matters worse, the fourth finger then has to stretch up to the 9th fret while still sustaining the other notes!

One more position shift is needed in bar twenty-three. We are required to play several notes in one position, then a higher finger "bypasses" the index finger to reach a lower fret. Cellists are very good at this kind of leap, as they often play along the length of a single string, but the manoeuvre is less common for guitarists who typically have to work harder to achieve the necessary coordination.

Isolate the difficult movement by playing the 7th fret with your first finger, then release it as the fourth finger jumps to the 5th fret. Keep practising this motion until you can do it so quickly that there is almost no gap between the notes and the transition is as seamless as possible.

You will need to involve your whole arm in the position shift, so make you're completely relaxed. We could have played all six notes in the seventh position using the B string, but this way the open string chord can be sustained for the whole bar providing a thicker overall texture.

Diversions Op. 16, No. 6 – Matteo Carcassi

Open E major tuning

Grazioso

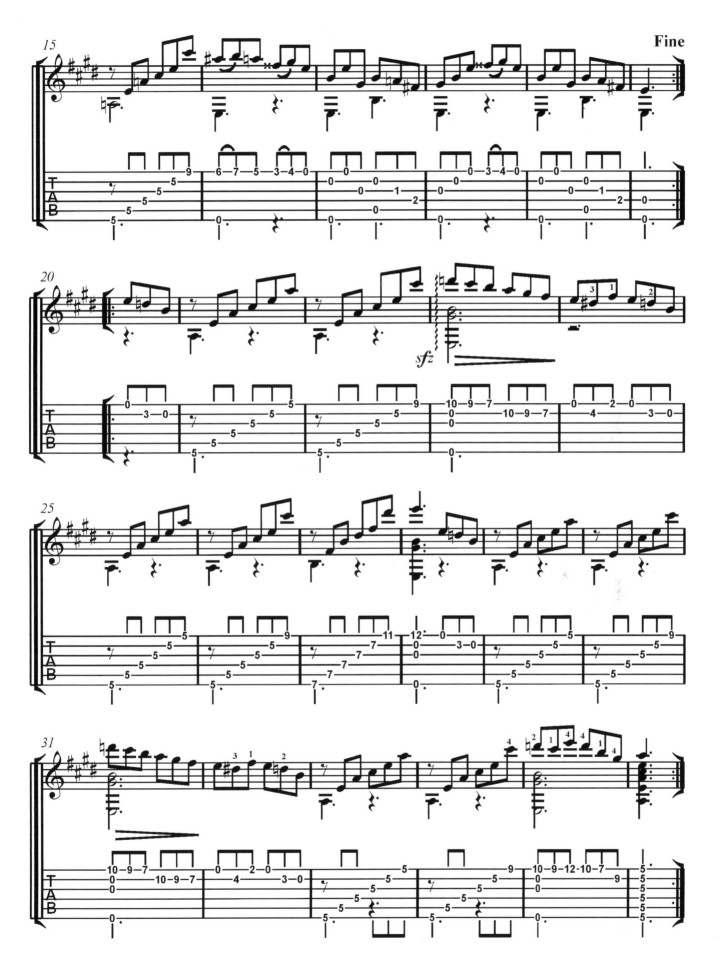

This page is intentionally left blank

15. Chorale – G.F. Handel
(arranged by Francisco Tárrega)

The next piece is a transcription of music written for choir by the Baroque period composer George Frederick Handel. The transcription is by Tárrega. Since the piece was originally written for groups of voices, the primary goal for this piece is to make each layer clear and distinct.

The tempo is slow throughout, but there are several uncommon chord shapes which will be difficult at first. When arranging music for guitar, the chord voicings are often a problem. For example, some options come naturally on piano due to the layout of the notes on the keyboard. Similarly, any arrangement of notes is possible in music written for voices.

This means that when transferring this music onto guitar, certain compromises must be made in order to make the chords playable. The original choral setting would have featured four voices, but most of the chord shapes have only three notes. Tárrega dispensed with the least important "inside voice" in each chord to make them more manageable and the transitions smoother. (An inside voice is one that sits in between the highest and lowest voices. For example the alto or tenor sit "inside" the soprano and bass). This is a good compromise as the highest and lowest parts are most easily discerned by the listener and are therefore more important to keep in the arrangement.

Play the A chord in bar four by barring your first finger. Keeping this finger in place will make the chord shapes easier during the next four bars. Arch your finger to play the open strings where necessary.

The slides in bars seven and eight will test your finger independence. Practise holding down the B7 barre chord in bar seven while moving the fourth finger back and forth between the E and D#. There should be no buzzes or deadening of the other three notes. Working on this level of fretting hand control will help your overall tone and dexterity, but is particularly helpful in this piece where sustaining each note is important.

The next trouble spot will likely be bar thirteen. Keep the D Major chord held down while using hammer-ons and pull-offs to play the melodic turn on the B string. To ease the hand into this and avoid tension, start by playing the legato phrase alone, then while barring the G and B strings with the first finger. Finally, add the third finger to complete the chord shape.

In bar twenty a similar turn occurs. This time it must be played with the second and fourth fingers, while the first holds down the D# bass note. Bar twenty-two features another slide within a chord and the advice for bar seven applies here too.

In bar thirty the second finger should fret the B string throughout. By using this as a reference point for each chord you will ensure smoother transitions and also prepare the correct fingering for the chord in bar thirty-one.

Once you are comfortable with the notes, start to think about the dynamics and pace of your performance. Subtle control of these nuances is what makes choral music so impactful, and it's this character you should aim to eventually emulate.

Chorale – G.F. Handel

This page is intentionally left blank

16. Bagatelle No. 3, Op. 4 – Heinrich Marschner

The third bagatelle from Heinrich Marschner's *Opus 4* is divided into two contrasting sections. The first is a proud, march-like idea in the key of A Major marked to be played "resolutely"!

The second half is in A Minor and features a long set of cascading arpeggios in a very Romantic style. The indication of *dolce* (literally "sweetly") suggests a reflective and mournful affectation that heightens the contrast with the bold A section.

However, the piece maintains a fast tempo throughout, so there will be plenty of technical obstacles to overcome before concerning yourself with the emotive performance directions.

The structure of the piece is confusing and Marschner's intention in the original score is ambiguous. After consulting several recordings here is what I feel is the most musically well-balanced option:

- Perform bars one to eight (A1) and bars nine to eighteen (A2) with the repeats as marked.

- Then return to the sign at bar one and play A1 again. This time, jump to the Coda at bar nineteen instead of repeating A1.

- Play bars nineteen to twenty-six (B1) and bars twenty-six to thirty-four (B2) with their repeats.

- After taking the second-time bar at the end of B2, return to the top to play A1, A2 and A1 once again, this time ignoring the repeat marks.

In the A section follow the fingering suggestions to help navigate the tricky bits. The startlingly dark sounding octave motif at the end of bar fourteen is best played using fingers one and four for the octaves and two for the E. The wrist will have to move up and down the neck slightly to accommodate both shapes. Use the second finger as an anchor point from which to pivot your hand.

As a general rule, alternate between different fingers to find the smoothest fingerings. The same finger shouldn't be used for consecutive notes on different strings unless this is absolutely unavoidable.

Look for notes that are common between the chords and leave your fingers held down where possible. If there are no common tones, then look for adjacent notes on the same string that the finger could slide to without lifting off. The fingerings I suggest throughout the book always observe these rules, resulting in the smoothest possible transitions.

After the strenuous A section, the B section is mercifully consistent. You should maintain a repetitive **p, i, m** pattern throughout, and as long as you keep a relaxed hand position, you should be able to increase the speed easily with consistent practice.

The fretting hand also has an easier time in the B section, with the exception of bars twenty-five and twenty-seven. Here, the chord shapes change on every beat of the bar, but the fingering suggestions mean they link together more naturally. Practise slowly, making the changes as smooth and gradual as possible.

Bagatelle No. 3, Op. 4 – Heinrich Marschner

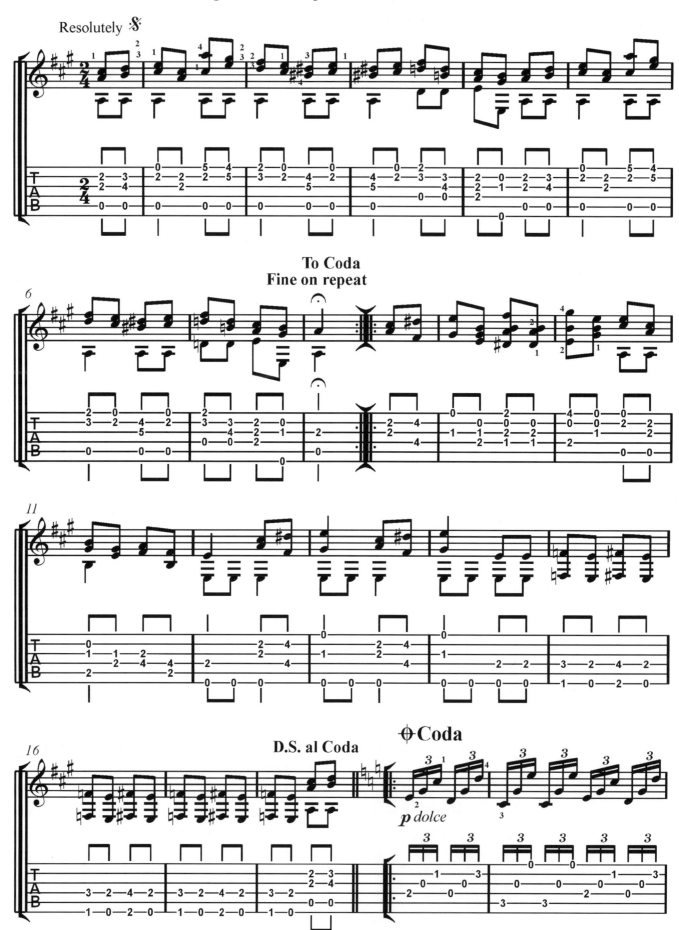

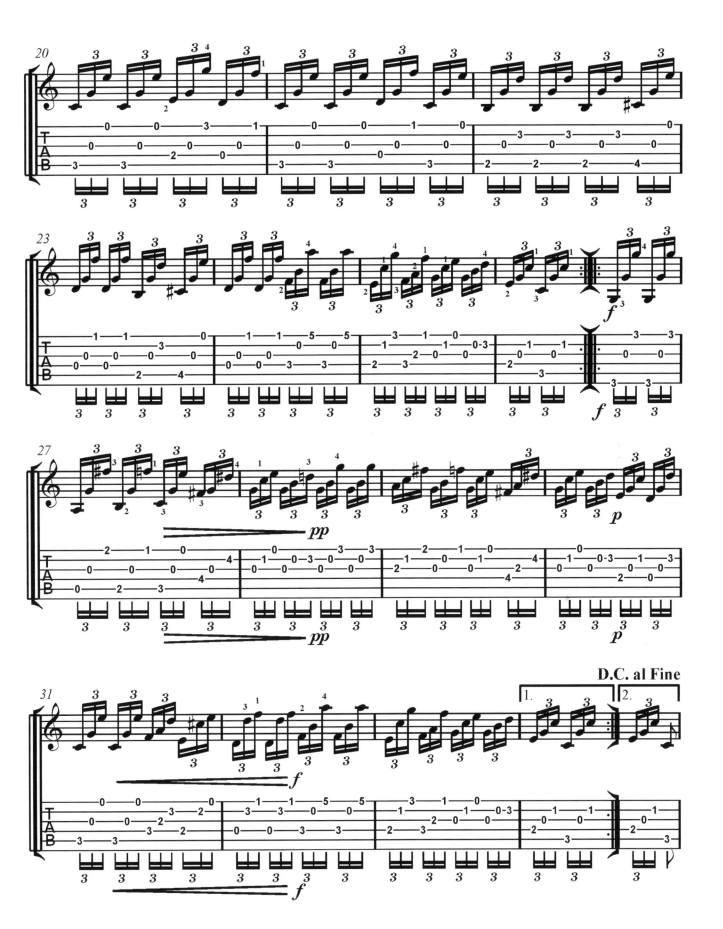

This page is intentionally left blank

17. Six Little Pieces Op. 19, No. 2 – Arnold Schoenberg
(arranged by Rob Thorpe)

Austrian composer Arnold Schoenberg (1874-1951) is remembered as the father of *atonality*. He was instrumental in shepherding classical music away from traditional chord progressions in the early twentieth century.

Atonal music dispenses with the idea that dissonance needs to resolve to consonance. Instead, the colour of each chord is allowed to be embraced on its own terms. Schoenberg felt that atonality was the natural development for the Germanic harmony of Wagner, Strauss and ultimately back to Bach.

This arrangement of one of Schoenberg's *Six Little Pieces* for piano is more abstract and textural than most of the repertoire in this book. Listen to a piano performance (I recommend Daniel Barenboim's recording) as well as the included audio. This will give you a better sense of how to phrase the piece.

The main motif is the repeating open string double-stop. These should always be short and detached, so bring the picking hand fingers back onto the strings after each pluck.

Bar three will need careful practice before the picking hand can multi-task. Focus on a single pluck and have **i** and **m** mute, while the low string rings out.

Pluck the harmonics in the same way, laying a fretting hand finger gently across the strings, directly over the fret. Ensure you're getting good harmonics by practising without muting to check they ring out properly. Fret the harmonics in bar five with your fourth finger. This may be unfamiliar at first, but will make the ensuing position shift much easier.

In bar two, play the first fretted notes with the second and fourth fingers, so the first finger is ready to play the next two notes which start the low melody. Use the open A string note to change position so that the D and G# notes can be played with the second and first fingers respectively.

As with our other transcriptions of keyboard pieces, several changes have been made. Most crucially, the octaves of several parts were altered to bring them into the playable range of the guitar.

The larger chords had to be edited down to avoid impossible fingerings. In the case of bar six, I chose to omit the D# from the seven-note chord to best reflect the original sound. Carefully follow the fingerings in the notation. The double-stop leading up to it should be slid down a fret, which sets up the rest of the chord.

The final phrase uses some more advanced techniques to allow the music to be as true to the original as possible. Follow the fingerings written in for the descending double-stops. These leave a convenient finger available each time to fret the 12th fret harmonic, while the hand continues to move down the fretboard.

The final chord uses another type of harmonic, known as an artificial harmonic. Perform it by pointing the picking hand index finger at the nineteenth fret of the low E string. Use the same gentle touch as when playing harmonics with the fretting hand. Now pluck the string with **p** to sound the harmonic.

Once this is comfortable, simultaneously pluck the A string with **m**. The G note should be played by barring the 10th fret with the first finger, in preparation for the rest of the final chord.

Six Little Pieces Op. 19, No. 2– Arnold Schoenberg

18. Ebb – Rob Thorpe
(arranged by Rob Thorpe)

Ebb is a composition taken from my band Polar Institute's debut album. The original is written for six musicians, so it was an interesting challenge to capture the essence of the piece in a solo guitar arrangement.

Structurally, the piece is rather simple. There are only two four-bar chord progressions. The first is in 4/4 in the key of C Major, over which several melodic ideas are layered. The piece then shifts dramatically at the musical climax, two thirds of the way through, into 3/4 time and the parallel key of C Minor.

The introduction contains some potentially awkward chord shapes. In order to sustain all the notes for their full rhythmic value, bars three and four have a challenging stretch to play the chord shape. In bar three, the first finger should handle all the notes on the top two strings. Your hand position may have to be altered from the initial chord shape to the final one, but be sure to keep the lower notes held down properly as you change.

In bar five, barring at the 7th fret saves an unnecessary adjustment for the next shape. The tempo in these opening phrases should be very expressive and rubato. Accelerate and crescendo on each two-bar phrase to give them more shape and character.

The tempo settles down when we reach the main repeating figure in bar nine, originally played on piano. It would be worth practising the repeating quaver pattern without the bassline while the thumb rests on the low E string, so you're not tempted to use it to pluck the melody.

This melodic line continued throughout the original piece, but sacrifices had to be made when creating the solo version, so for the next passage I've opted to combine the electric guitar part which alternated two notes on each chord with the vocal melody.

Much like the alternating-bass approach we saw in the folk inspired piece *Newport Fair*, breaking down the two parts separately before eventually combining them will pay dividends. When it comes time to play both the top and bottom lines together, tackle it one bar at a time. Get to know which beat of the bar the melody falls on and count through very slowly in order to commit it to muscle memory.

As before, you should use your thumb for all the low notes from bars seventeen onwards, with the possible exception of bars twenty-one and twenty-two. Here the wide string skipping might prove too awkward and a combination of **p** and **i** be more preferable.

The repeating motif then becomes the high texture, so alternate **i** and **m** while brushing the bass chords with the thumb.

The key change at bar 41 to C Minor is less suited to the guitar's open strings than C Major, so maintaining the moving bass motif becomes problematic. (I changed the key from the original G Major for this reason). The repeating bass note is now on the offbeat to maintain the sense of energy. Even with this reduction, to give a convincing performance the fingerings will need to be carefully thought out and practised.

There have been some challenging contortions so far for the fretting hand, but now the picking hand gets a workout. At bar forty-five the picking hand settles into a repetitive fast rolling pattern. Along with the preceding section, this forms the climax of the piece, so you'll need to practise maintaining a strong attack and volume for the whole section. The fretting hand only needs to keep the chord shapes held down, but the changes need to be quick and tidy to avoid disrupting the flow.

Ebb (arrangement) – Rob Thorpe

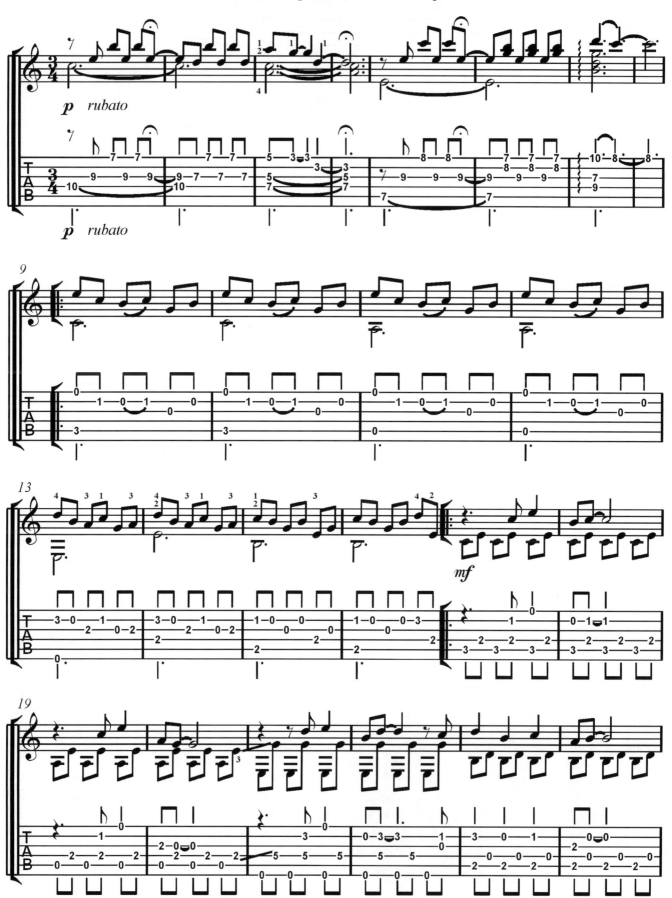

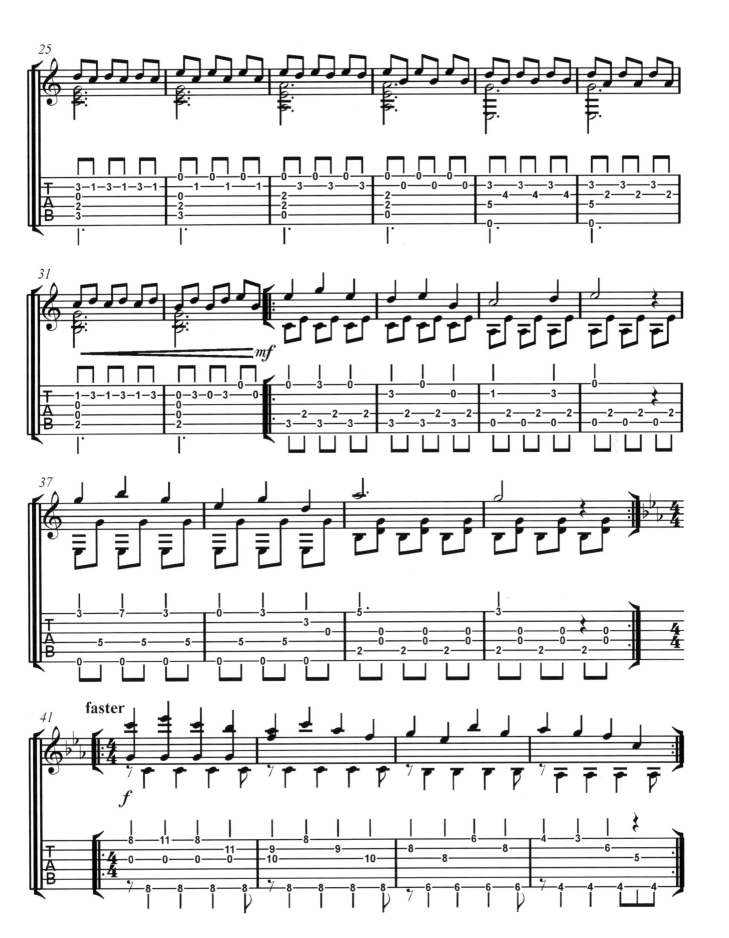

19. Prelude No. 20 – Frederik Chopin
(arranged by Francisco Tárrega)

The Polish composer and pianist Frederik Chopin needs little introduction. His music has remained very popular and is as much loved now as it ever was. Almost all of Chopin's output was composed for solo piano. His collection of preludes follows in the tradition begun by Bach of writing twenty-four preludes using each of the major and minor keys. Later Scriabin, Debussy and Shostakovich would all write similar sets.

The pieces by Bach and Haydn in this book would have been played on harpsichord, but by 1800 the pianoforte (also known as the *hammerklavier*) had become more prevalent. This new instrument afforded musicians the ability to vary the volume of each note, unlike the harpsichord. By Chopin's time, the piano had opened a whole new world of musical expression in keyboard music, which made possible the dramatic music of the nineteenth century's Romantic composers.

The piano is capable of playing more simultaneous notes than the guitar and its range is almost four octaves wider. Therefore, we have to make some compromises to the original music, mainly in the bass notes and certain chord voicings. Thankfully, with some clever arrangements, we guitarists can enjoy Chopin's pieces too. Like the Haydn *Minuet*, Chopin's *Prelude No. 20* was transcribed for guitar by Francisco Tárrega, so we're in safe hands.

Prelude No. 20 is written in the key of C Minor. Some of the chord voicings may be new to you, so each bar is worthy of focused attention before attempting to connect phrases together.

The tempo is very slow. Although the piece is a mere thirteen bars long, it should take about 1 minute and 20 seconds to perform. While this gives you plenty of thinking time in the learning stage, it will also test your stamina for holding some of the more taxing barre chords.

Watch out for the first chord in bar five. Plucking the D string with **i** creates a gap between it and the other fingers which can feel awkward at first.

When playing a slow-moving, dramatic piece like this, it can be tempting to rake through the chords to give a flamenco-esque flourish, but this sound quickly becomes over-used. Opt to pluck the whole chord simultaneously with all four digits, except for the moments where an arpeggio is signalled by the vertical wavy line before the chords, as in bars four and thirteen. In these instances, use the thumb to rake across strings so there is a slight delay between the attack of each string. Use the audio as a reference if you're unsure.

Once the chord shapes are coming together, you'll want to address the melody that connects the top notes of each chord. For example, in bar five focus on keeping the fourth finger held down on the 12th then 11th fret, while the other fingers change to fret each chord. To help with the more unpredictable fingerings I've placed numbers over the notation to show the most fluid approaches.

Prelude No. 20 – Frederik Chopin

20. Prelude in C, BWV 846 – J.S. Bach

(arranged by Rob Thorpe)

Finally, we return to the Baroque period for some J.S. Bach. The *Prelude in C* is from Bach's set of twenty-four preludes and fugues for the "Well-Tempered Clavier". It's one of his most enduring and popular compositions, so makes for a well-received performance piece.

The collection's full title refers not to an affable piano, but instead to the then relatively new concept of equal temperament. Equal temperament is the modern tuning system used in Western European music, which approximates the true or *just* intervals, so that all twelve semitones are equally spaced. This development allowed for every key to be played without retuning and Baroque composers soon started to exploit the ability to modulate between keys many times during a piece.

Prelude in C is composed by taking a single arpeggiation pattern and applying it to a long chord progression.

The piece starts and ends on the familiar open C Major chord, but in between the harmony moves slowly away from the home chord by introducing increasing amounts of tension.

Several of the chords are quite uncommon and demanding. For example, bar five requires two simultaneous barres and a wide stretch. Placing the fingers gradually as you play each note will help you form awkward shapes, rather than changing to the whole chord straight away.

As well as contending with each shape individually, you should consider how effective the transitions between chords are. In bar ten, the D7 chord should be played with the second, third and fourth fingers. Though this might feel unnatural at first, the change from bar nine and then into bar eleven will be easier.

Bars twenty-eight to thirty will test your fretting hand strength as the first finger should remain barred across the 5th fret throughout, while the other fingers change chord. Squeeze the neck as little as possible with your thumb, without getting any buzzing notes, and keep relaxed. With optimal finger placement surprisingly little force is needed for barre chords.

As with the arrangement of Handel's *Chorale* and Chopin's *Prelude No. 20*, adjustments were needed at several points in this piece to make the chords physically possible on guitar. The chords in bar sixteen onwards have been moved up an octave. The priority when arranging a piece of music is to preserve its overall identity. In this case that meant sustaining the bass note and allowing all the notes to ring out as much as possible.

Bach's compositions rarely had dynamic or tempo markings in the original manuscripts. While some publishers later added them, I've chosen to present the score without them, so you are free to interpret the piece your own way.

Prelude in C, BWV 846 – J.S. Bach

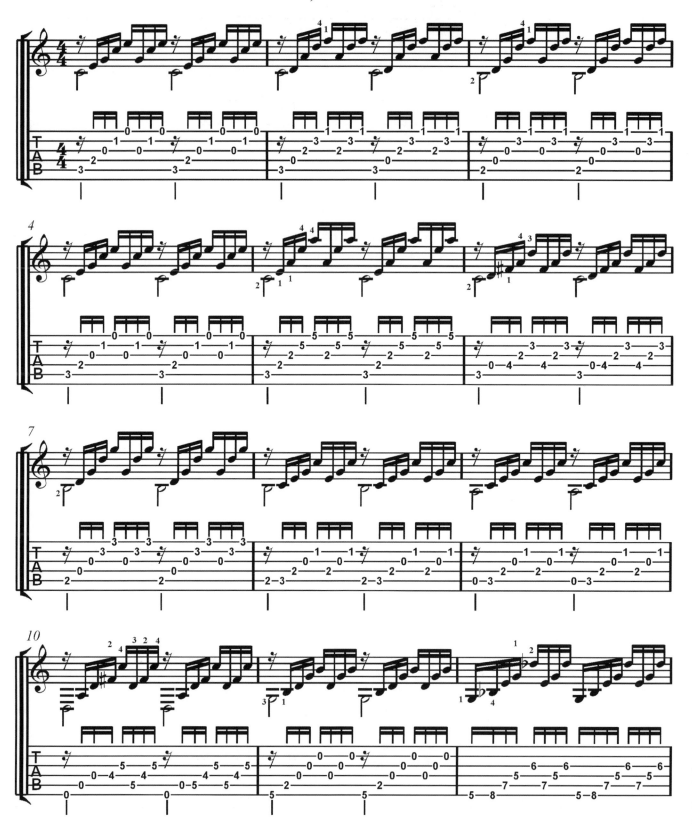

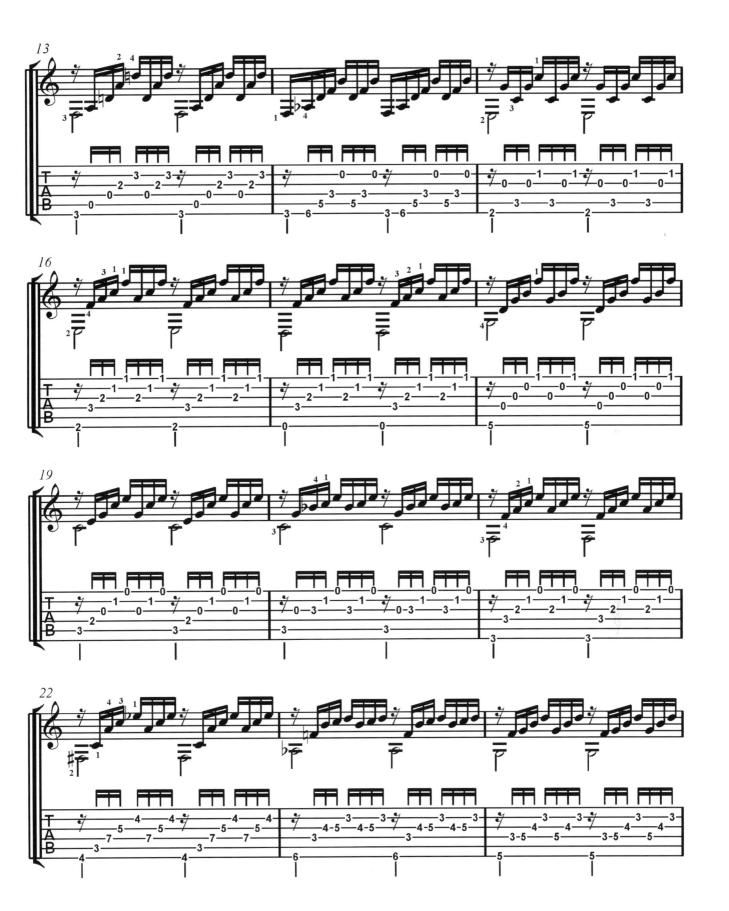

Closing Words

Having worked through the pieces I've presented here, I encourage you to go and explore other works by the composers whose music you've most enjoyed. The skills you've developed here should allow you to unlock more challenging pieces to add to your repertoire.

Over the course of these books I've included a range of music from different periods, starting with Baroque, then Classical, then the Romantic period, as well as some folk-inspired pieces. It is interesting to observe the similarities that occur in pieces from each era, as well as how much guitar playing has developed over the course of four centuries.

It's important to listen widely and critically to train your ear to discern the nuances of the great players. Hearing the subtle details in music will also help you appreciate a much wider range of styles.

To discover more music, you should seek out recordings of music from the Romantic era and twentieth century composers and guitarists. Below are some recommendations for further listening. These will inform all aspects of fingerpicking, as they include music from the Baroque and Classical periods as well as that of modern singer-songwriters.

- John Dowland – *Galliard* (solo lute)
- J.S. Bach – *Air on a G String*
- Joseph Küffner – *25 Sonatines for Guitar op. 80*
- Edvard Grieg – *Hall of the Mountain King*
- Nicolo Paganini – *Sonatina No. 1*
- Isaac Albéniz – *Leyenda (Asturias)*
- Francisco Tárrega – *Recuerdos de la Alhambra*
- Heitor Villa-Lobos – *Study No. 1 "Prelude"*
- Francisco Mignone – *12 Waltzes for Guitar*
- Stanley Myers/John Williams – *Cavatina (Theme from The Deer Hunter)*
-
- Michael Hedges – *Aerial Boundaries*
- Pierre Bensusan - *Voyage for Ireland*
- David Mead – *Nocturnal*
- Steve Howe – *The Clap*
- Steve Morse – *Coast to Coast*

  Nick Drake – *Cello Song*
- James Taylor – *Something in the Way She Moves*
- Eva Cassidy – *Songbird*
- Metallica – *Nothing Else Matters*

I hope you've enjoyed playing these pieces and felt the satisfaction that comes from learning to play complete pieces of music you're then able to perform to others. Keep returning to these pieces and fine tune your technique and performance. You will grow as a musician and discover new dimensions to add to enhance the tunes.

Good luck with the next stage of your guitar playing journey.

Rob Thorpe

Other Books from Fundamental Changes

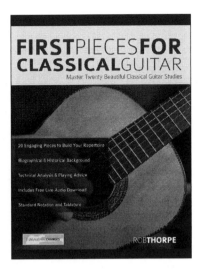

Master 20 Beautiful Classical Guitar Pieces for Beginners

First Pieces for Classical Guitar features 20 carefully selected pieces – each written by a past master of the instrument – aimed at beginners who want to learn to play entire, beautiful pieces. The natural progression of the studies from beginner to intermediate will help you develop your classical guitar language quickly and easily. Notation is included, but each piece is also presented in easy-to-read tablature, so an ability to read music is not necessary.

- 20 beautiful, incremental classical guitar studies
- Playing advice and a breakdown of each classical guitar piece
- Perfectly notated music and guitar tablature with studio-quality audio to download for free.

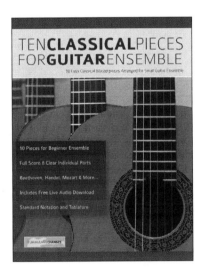

10 Beautiful Classical Pieces Specially Arranged for Guitar Ensemble

Ten Classical Pieces for Guitar Ensemble features 10 well-known, much-loved classical pieces. Together they make up a satisfying performance repertoire for small groups of guitarist to play together. It is often difficult to find works by the great composers written specifically for guitar ensemble, so this book is an essential resource for teachers and students alike.

- 10 pieces of famous classical music, specially transcribed and arranged for small groups of guitarists playing as an ensemble
- Presented in easy-to-read tablature and notation. No need to read music
- Each piece includes a teacher's score and individual parts for 3-4 guitarists

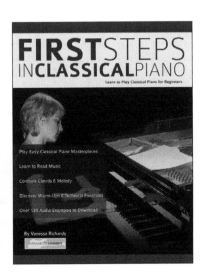

Take Your First Steps in Classical Piano Playing

First Steps in Classical Piano is the beginning of your journey to playing beautiful classical piano pieces. Either as a stand-alone guide, or as a resource to support lessons with your piano teacher, First Steps in Classical Piano will dramatically speed up how you learn to play piano. You will quickly master excerpts from iconic classical piano pieces, while learning to read music, play scales and develop piano technique.

- A step-by-step explanation of correct piano technique
- Warm-up exercises at the beginning of each chapter
- Carefully chosen excerpts from the best-loved classical piano pieces

Made in United States
Orlando, FL
28 November 2023

39562743R00046